ABIDING

A Journey Through The Vines and Branches of John 15

Eric B Summers

ABIDING : A Journey Through The Vines and Branches of John 15

Copyright © 2025 by Eric B Summers

All rights reserved. Printed in the United States of America. No part of this book may be used or reproduced in any manner whatsoever without written permission.

Scripture quotations are from the ESV Bible (The Holy Bible, English Standard Version), 2001 by Crossway, a publishing ministry of Good News Publishers. ESV Text Edition: 2025. The ESV text may not be quoted in any publication made available to the public by a Creative Commons License. The ESV may not be translated in whole or in part into any other language. Used by permission. All rights reserved.

ISBN: 978-1-968112-95-0

Printed in USA

Table Of Contents

Introduction *5*
Chapter 1 God as the Vinedresser *7*
Chapter 2 Abide In His Life *11*
Chapter 3 Grafted in Love *17*
Chapter 4 Abiding In His Love *20*
Chapter 5 Thriving In Jesus *26*
Chapter 6 Abide In His Name *30*
About the Author *37*
Acknowledgments *38*

Introduction

This book is the output of a series from our Wednesday night student ministry environment called the REVOLUTION. I had a book study scheduled for the end of the season before summer, and in my own quiet times I came across John 15. This metaphor taught by Jesus resonated with me so well, and I couldn't get past it. So, I developed this series around the idea of what it means to "abide" in Jesus. The students connected so well with the metaphor and had great conversations in their small groups.

The way the material is designed to work is based on our student environment. The night would begin with a short lesson based on John 15 and then we would split off into small groups to have a much deeper discussion on the material. The book you hold in your hand is a combination of my teaching notes and the discussion guides I created for the small group leaders each week. There is a chapter that come from the teaching notes, and then the following material is pulled from the small group discussion guides. Together they build on each other and develop this beautiful metaphor that Jesus uses to show us what it means to abide in Him.

Chapter 1
God as the Vinedresser

In John 15, Jesus introduces a metaphor that would be easily understood by His audience. The culture He was teaching in revolved around agricultural lifestyles and to His audience, the source of life coming through a vine would be powerful and evident. But this isn't the first time that God would use this metaphor to explain His relationship to His people. Jesus connects to the message from the Prophet Isaiah that uses the vine metaphor to explain God's relationship with His chosen people. Let's look at that passage now:

"Let me sing for my beloved
   my love song concerning his vineyard:
My beloved had a vineyard
   on a very fertile hill.
He dug it and cleared it of stones,
   and planted it with choice vines;
he built a watchtower in the midst of it,
   and hewed out a wine vat in it;
and he looked for it to yield grapes,
   but it yielded wild grapes.
And now, O inhabitants of Jerusalem
   and men of Judah,
judge between me and my vineyard.
What more was there to do for my vineyard,
   that I have not done in it?
When I looked for it to yield grapes,
   why did it yield wild grapes?
And now I will tell you
   what I will do to my vineyard.
I will remove its hedge,

>   and it shall be devoured;
> I will break down its wall,
>   and it shall be trampled down.
> I will make it a waste;
>   it shall not be pruned or hoed,
>   and briers and thorns shall grow up;
> I will also command the clouds
>   that they rain no rain upon it.
> For the vineyard of the Lord of hosts
>   is the house of Israel,
> and the men of Judah
>   are his pleasant planting;
> and he looked for justice,
>   but behold, bloodshed;
> for righteousness,
>   but behold, an outcry!"
> -Isaiah 5:1-7 (ESV)

In this passage from Isaiah, God is the vinedresser. He's the person tending the vineyard and He gives the vineyard every possible advantage to thrive. It's a no-brainer that it should bear good fruit. He established the vineyard on fertile ground, starting with a productive foundation. He cleared the ground of stones before carefully planting only the best vines. He surrounded it with a protective hedge and built a watchtower in the middle so He could oversee the growth. He even built a wine vat in anticipation of a great harvest. But as we keep reading, the vineyard doesn't produce what was desired, instead it took all those advantages and produced wild, unwanted fruit.

God then destroys the vineyard; He takes away the things protecting the vineyard and all the things helping it to grow. As this passage closes out, we see the metaphor explained. The vineyard was the nation of Israel, chosen as God's own people. He had given them every benefit and set them up to thrive, only to have their sinful choices produce bad fruit. God had done miraculous things for Israel, crossing rivers on dry ground, manna falling from heaven, water pouring from a rock in the desert, and still they turned their back on God. He allows enemies to capture Israel at various times in their history. They were forced to endure the consequences of their choices. Why do you think Jesus built off this metaphor when speaking to the crowd in John 15?

I think there are two main reasons, the first is that the crowd was Jewish and would have been very familiar with this metaphor. They had been taught this passage since their birth, and it was easily understood. The second reason is more meaningful and connects us to the story. Jesus was showing the crowd that where Israel failed in obedience, Jesus was the fulfillment. He would be the new vineyard and would produce the good fruit that God intended Isreal to produce. Jesus used this metaphor to bridge from the old covenant to the new covenant that He was establishing. No longer did we have to be the source of goodness, Jesus was now the source. His goodness is what we are measured by, not our own. That really is "good news."

As we move into John 15, Jesus is telling us how to live our lives properly connected to the source. Like branches grafted into a healthy plant, we can't bear fruit without being connected to our source, Jesus!

Chapter 2
Abide In His Life

In this first section of John 15 we are looking at what it means to be connected to Jesus' Life. He focuses on this image of a vine and its branches. *What part of the illustration is Jesus? What part do we play when we have been saved? What part does God play?*

What purpose does a branch serve? Does it provide structure for the whole plant? No, the branch is there to produce fruit. The water and nutrients come from the vine, not from the branch. There is a complex system in plants where nutrients and water are carried back and forth between the branches and the core of the plant. Jesus chose this illustration as His listeners would be familiar with vineyards and plants. He is trying to communicate that apart from Him, we are fruitless and useless. To bear fruit in our lives and to live out our days in a meaningful way, we MUST be connected to the source, which is Him.

Jesus doesn't waste much time before He gets to a tough point. Have someone reread **verse 2**. *What is pruning when we are talking about plants?*

Pruning in the agricultural sense is when you cut away branches to promote more fruit in other branches or you cut away branches that are not producing fruit. In both cases you are limiting the amount of nutrients that are getting pulled away from the productive parts of the plant. *Knowing that, what is Jesus talking about when says that God is the vinedresser and is pruning branches?* We can probably understand why you would cut off branches that are dead from a plant, but when we take that to a spiritual level, it gets heavy. *Why would God want to remove spiritually unfruitful people from the vineyard? What does that say about their salvation to begin with?*

God doesn't cut people off that have genuinely surrendered their lives to Jesus. Scripture is beyond clear about that. Even when we sin, even when we mess up big, even when we run from God in our shame, He is still faithful to us. But there are also other passages of Scripture that talk about people who pretend to be Christians and can convince a lot of people but are just playing a game. Those are the fruitless branches that God will prune to give the healthy branches the best chance to grow.

There is another level to this illustration as well. A vinedresser doesn't just prune the dead branches, he would also prune some healthy branches to help them produce more fruit.

Pruning isn't always cutting off, sometimes it's cutting back to force the branch to grow. To connect this back to the life of a believer, there will be times in our lives when God will allow us to face trouble to help us grow and bear more fruit. Those times aren't fun, but God is with us in those prunings and He's doing it because He loves us and knows we have more inside of us than we think. Two verses that come to mind when in a season of pruning are **Romans 5:3-5** and James **1:2-4**, read both together in your group.

"Not only that, but we rejoice in our sufferings, knowing that suffering produces endurance, and endurance produces character, and character produces hope, and hope does not put us to shame, because God's love has been poured into our hearts through the Holy Spirit who has been given to us." (ESV, Romans 5:3-5)

"Count it all joy, my brothers, when you meet trials of various kinds, for you know that the testing of your faith produces steadfastness. And let steadfastness have its full effect, that you may be perfect and complete, lacking in nothing." (James 1:2-4)

Believers are not promised a comfortable life free from hardship, Scripture is clear that we will face hard times, we just have a hope that is bigger than us. *Why do you think God allows us to go through hardships in our lives? Wouldn't it be more loving to just fix everything for us and not make us suffer? What would we miss out on if God chose that way?*

Suffering produces strength in us, strength that can't be earned any other way. So, part of our experiencing Jesus' life is that we must experience a small part of His suffering as well as God prunes our lives.

There is another part of this passage I want us to look at and that's **verse 5**. *What does Jesus say here?* When we abide in Jesus, we will produce much fruit. The verse doesn't stop there, what comes next? "Apart from Me you can do nothing." *How does that phrase sit with you? Anyone have issue with it? Why do you think we naturally get defensive when we are told we can't do anything?*

We put a lot of weight in what we can do, a lot of our identity and our self-worth rests on accomplishments and to be told without hesitation that we can't do anything on our own, it's hard to hear.

But when we step back from the emotions and look at what Jesus is saying, it's not an attack on our worth, it's really a confirmation that we need Jesus to be who we were made to be.

We can still do the day-to-day stuff, but to be fully "us" we need Jesus at the center of it all. We operate at our best with Jesus in the middle, we are led into God's plans for our lives when Jesus is in the middle, and we will find the best results in our lives when Jesus is at the center of them. *There are plenty of successful people that don't know Jesus, how does that work into this conversation?* The success of the world is not the success of the Kingdom. Which are we serving with our lives? We might find great success in the worlds eyes by being selfish, unethical, or unbalanced in our work lives, but what have we really gained? **Mark 8:36-37** speaks to this. Read it together.

"For what does it profit a man to gain the whole world and forfeit his soul? For what can a man give in return for his soul?" (Mark 8:36-37)

What does success look like for a believer?

Who should get recognition for success in the life of a believer? (Hint, **John 15:8**)

As we finish up this first section of John 15, we must remember that our best results will only come when we are attached to the source, Jesus. We will face times of pruning in life, but those moments remind us that the vinedresser sees more potential in us, and we will make it through them!

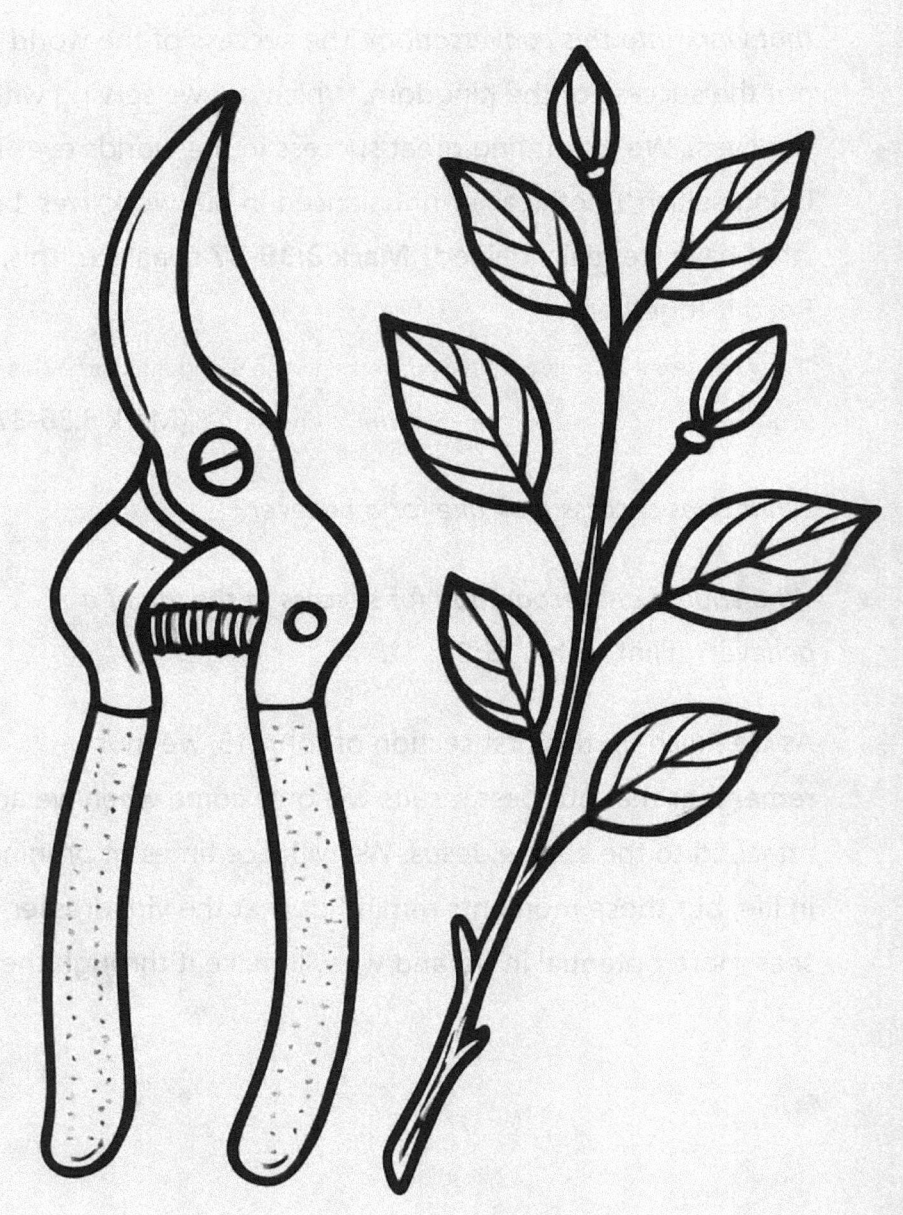

Chapter 3
Grafted in Love

Before we get back to John 15, I want to dig a little deeper into the plant metaphor that Jesus is teaching through. Keep in mind that Jesus was part of the creative process in Genesis 1 so all the natural systems that are in play in creation were designed and implemented by Jesus. There is an amazing cycle in plants that use two very specific cell types. Those cells are called Xylem and Phloem. They are both crucial to plant health and life cycles. The Xylem cells move water with dissolved nutrients from the root to the rest of the plant. The Phloem cells take sugars produced in the leaves after photosynthesis and moves them back to the roots. The exchange keeps the plant growing and fed. It's a perfectly balanced system just as God designed it.

These cells travel just below the bark which allows gardeners to graft plants. A graft is where you take part of another plant, in the same genus, and connect it to a different root system. The two types of plant will share xylem and phloem, and the transplanted piece will begin to grow as it is assimilated into the root plant. A lot of the modern fruits and vegetables we have on our tables have come to be because of grafting in the past.

Jump with me to Romans 11 and let's see how Paul uses an agricultural metaphor to explain how Gentiles are brought into God's family.

"But if some of the branches were broken off, and you, although a wild olive shoot, were grafted in among the others and now share in the nourishing root of the olive tree, do not be arrogant toward the branches. If you are, remember it is not you who support the root, but the root that supports you. Then you will say, "Branches were broken off so that I might be grafted in." That is true. They were broken off because of their unbelief, but you stand fast through faith. So do not become proud, but fear. For if God did not spare the natural branches, neither will he spare you. Note then the kindness and the severity of God: severity toward those who have fallen, but God's kindness to you, provided you continue in his kindness. Otherwise, you too will be cut off. And even they, if they do not continue in their unbelief, will be grafted in, for God has the power to graft them in again. For if you were cut from what is by nature a wild olive tree, and grafted, contrary to nature, into a cultivated olive tree, how much more will these, the natural branches, be grafted back into their own olive tree." (Romans 11:17-24)

In this passage, the olive tree symbolizes God's covenant with Israel. The natural branches were Jews, and the grafted branches were the Gentiles. The process of grafting in branches was God expanding His covenant to the rest of the world. As Gentiles, we get to experience His plan and blessings because of Jesus. Paul warns Gentiles to not look down on Jews because they are the root of God's promise and even those branches pruned away can be grafted back in if they get past their unbelief regarding Jesus. We have talked in John 15 about abiding with Jesus, the olive tree metaphor in Paul's letter explains the way we can live this out. God, in His mercy, grafted us into the family just like a donor limb is grafted into a sturdy root system.

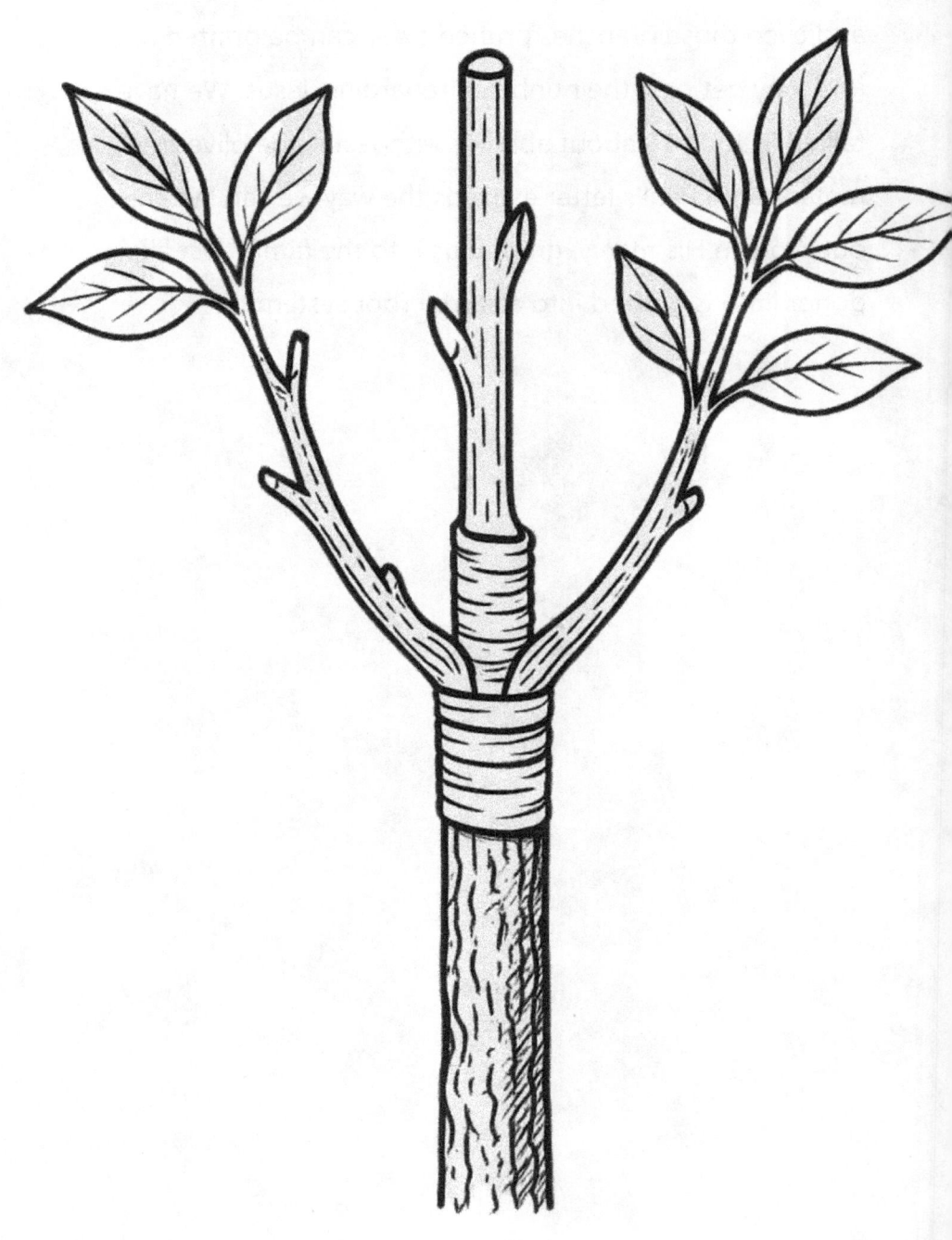

Chapter 4
Abiding In His Love

Earlier we talked about how important it was that we were connected to the source which is Jesus. We talked about pruning in our lives, sometimes to cut off dead branches and sometimes to help healthy branches bear more fruit. Remind the group, *what do the fruitless branches represent?* (People either pretending to be saved, or people thinking their goodness is enough) *What does it mean when we talk about healthy branches being pruned?* (That's when God allows tough seasons in our lives to make us stronger in our faith and able to bear more spiritual fruit.)

Now we are going to talk about the second part of "abiding" in Jesus and that's how we abide in His Love. Let's start off by reading **John 15:9-17** together.

"As the Father has loved me, so have I loved you. Abide in my love. If you keep my commandments, you will abide in my love, just as I have kept my Father's commandments and abide in his love. These things I have spoken to you, that my joy may be in you, and that your joy may be full. "This is my commandment, that you love one another as I have loved you. Greater love has no one than this, that someone lay down his life for his friends. You are my friends if you do what I command you. No longer do I call you servants, for the servant does not know what his master is doing; but I have called you friends, for all that I have heard from my Father I have made known to you. You did not choose me, but I chose you and appointed you that you should go and bear fruit and that your fruit should abide, so that whatever you ask the Father in my name, he may give it to you. These things I command you, so that you will love one another." (John 15:9-17)

 Pay attention to how many times "abide" is used in this section (4 in the ESV). *How many times is "love" used?* (9 in the ESV). *What standard does Jesus give us for how He loves us?* As the Father loves Him, if you pull up the Greek translation, that is Agape love, which means it's unconditional. There is nothing we can do to get God to love us more, and there is nothing we can do to make God love us less. His love for us is full, perfect, and complete. Jesus calls us to "abide in His love." What does that mean? Sounds great, harder to put into practical terms though. Jesus gives us some insight; we abide in His love when we obey His commandments. Is this a mindless obedience? I don't think so, instead I think about when someone we really care about asks us to do something. We do it, because we love that person and want to show them how much by doing what they ask. We don't do it to get love in return, we just want to show that person they are important to us, so we obey.

Jesus modeled this obedience for us in how He followed God's commands during His time on earth. That obedience brings us joy. Joy because we avoid things that are hurtful to us, and joy because we are showing God how much we love Him. Joy is a hard thing to find today, what word do people often mix up with joy? Happiness! Are they the same? Not at all. Happiness depends on the situations you are facing and what emotional place you are in at the time. Joy comes from outside of your situation and has nothing to do with your emotions. Abiding in Christ will allow us to have joy, even in tough times, because we know the most important relationship we have, our relationship with God, is secure and never up in the air.

Once we know our relationship with God is good, we can then begin to love others as Jesus commands us to. The next section of this passage turns our attention to others and is a very convicting piece of Scripture. Have someone reread **John 15:12-13** to the group. *What is this verse saying*? Most people jump to the extreme where we sacrifice our lives for other people, like push them out of the road in front of a bus or something. While that is heroic, there is a much more subtle and honestly more difficult application to this command. Laying down our life for others means that we lay down control and lay down our desires for the other person. In a short sentence, we sacrifice what we want for what they want. That is horribly difficult to live out, but Jesus showed it to perfection. His prayer in the Garden, something we read during Holy Week, is a perfect example. Have someone read **Matthew 26:38-44**. Jesus knew that His death was coming, it was a heavy burden to carry, but He also knew the Father's Will and that His sacrifice was the only way to deal with humanities sin problem. The way He worded His prayers to the Father demonstrate what He said in John 15. We must love even when it costs us. It's easy to love when we are getting things in return, the true measure of maturity is in how we love when it costs us something.

This part of the reading closes out with Jesus again calling us to love one another with a sacrificial love and an unconditional love. People that love this way, are not only willing to give up their wants for others, but they are also not quick to fight with each other. When you are loving others like Jesus, drama should be rare in those relationships. When there is a lot of drama in relationships, it really means there are a lot of people demanding their own way instead of loving others. That's a very hard truth to internalize, but when you can put that into practice, it will take you up a big notch in maturity and emotional health. *How can you be a peacemaker in your friend group? How would you explain this concept to a lost friend? What about those friends that thrive on drama, we all have them, how does this passage of Scripture impact your interactions with them?*

The main idea for this entire passage and series is that we find practical ways to abide, or dwell, in Jesus daily. Last week we talked about being connected to the source and then understanding the role that pruning has in the life of a healthy vine. This week we looked at how abiding in the love of Jesus will help us live out His commands in this life. Those commands aren't meant to keep us from having fun, instead they keep us from getting burned by our own sinful choices. They also help us make sure we are loving other people as we should. *Do you feel like the world/culture sees that point when we talk about obeying God? What do they think of instead?* Brainstorm on one way you can help the lost world see that living in the love of Jesus will make everything better.

Here is where it gets tough! There is probably someone at church or at school that you have an issue with, and you have not been loving them like Jesus would love them. If you are up for the challenge and really want to take a step to abide in Christ, I want you to reach out with a call, text, or note and apologize to that person. You can give as little or as much info as you want, but this is you, stepping into a hard spot, to love like Jesus. **John 13:35**

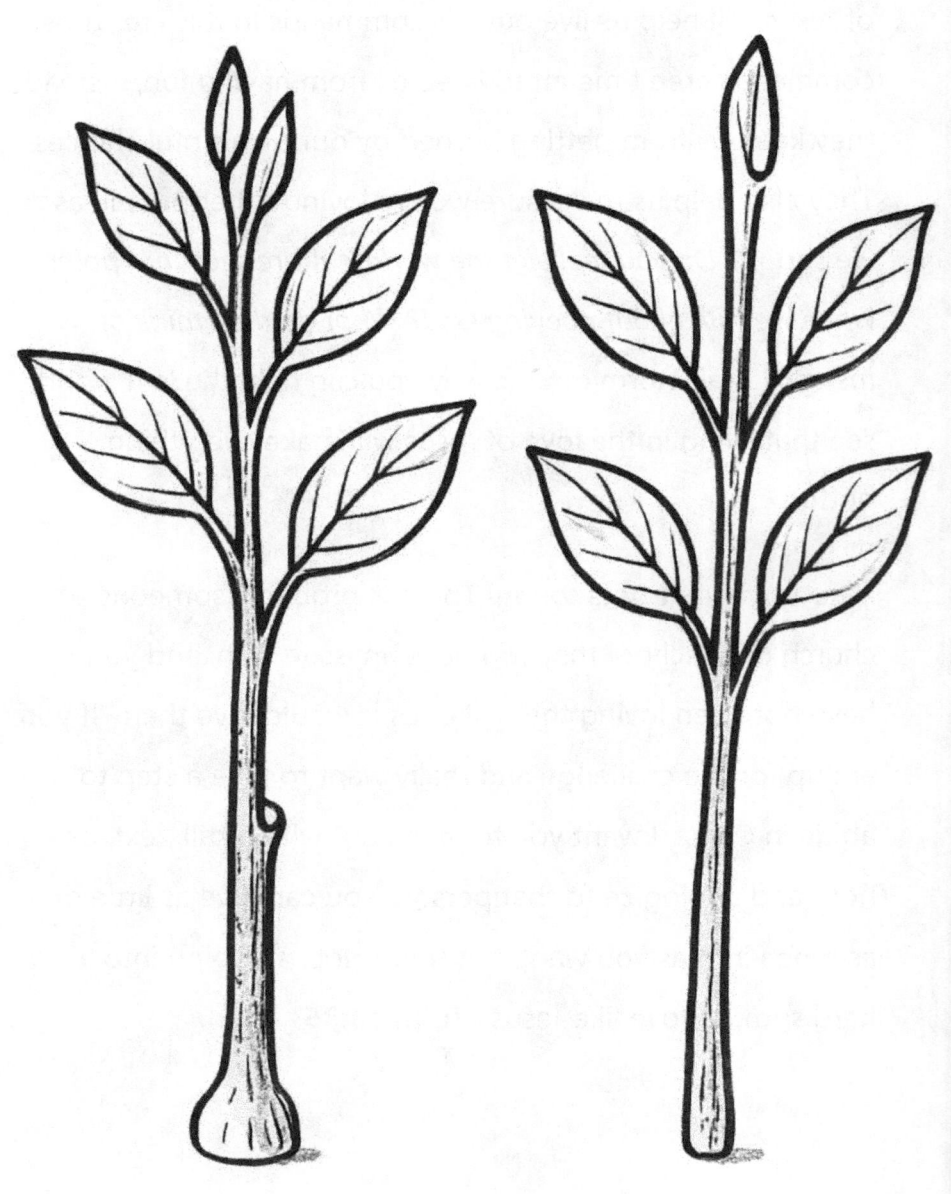

Chapter 5
Thriving In Jesus

We have unpacked this agricultural metaphor used by Jesus in John 15 and have seen how gardening practices can speak into our spiritual lives through this teaching. We have talked about pruning and its place in our spiritual growth. We have also talked about how we have been grafted into the family of God through Jesus. In this last section of John 15 we are going to look at one more aspect of grafting. When you are grafting a plant, the small part you are putting into the stable root system is called the scion. In our earlier conversation we know that if we were to perform a cleft graft where you split the stem of the host plant and split the stem of the scion and then wedge them together, the exchange of nutrients can feed the scion. Imagine you have two scions in front of you on the table. Both of the same plant, both equally as healthy when you clipped them. The first scion you are going to prepare carefully, get a good graft site, and after connecting to the host, you are going to wrap that graft with plant tape to be sure it holds, and the connection is healthy. The other scion, you are going to just leave on the table and not attach it to a root system. Which scion will thrive? Obviously, the one grafted to the host plant. Now I know some of you botany minded people will mention things like hydroponics or even aeroponics and you can look those up on Google on your own time, both of those processes can sustain a plant, but it requires so much effort and labor from the gardener. Those practices don't play into the metaphor we are using here.

The scion grafted to the host plant will survive and grow because of its connection to the xylem and phloem of the supporting plant. It will get the nutrients it needs through that exchange. The other clipping, the one left on the table to its own devices, will quickly shrivel up and die. It cannot survive unsupported. *Do you see now how this connects to our spiritual lives?*

When we "abide" in Jesus, we are grafted into the life-giving power of the Holy Spirit. The Early Church talks about our connection to the Holy Spirit a lot. Romans 8:9-11 talks about how the Holy Spirit restores our sin deadend hearts to life. He sustains us where our own efforts would just lead to more sin and death.

In Ephesians 3:14-19 Paul is praying for believers to be grafted into God's love through the Holy Spirit inside of us.

"For this reason I bow my knees before the Father, from whom every family in heaven and on earth is named, that according to the riches of his glory he may grant you to be strengthened with power through his Spirit in your inner being, so that Christ may dwell in your hearts through faith—that you, being rooted and grounded in love, may have strength to comprehend with all the saints what is the breadth and length and height and depth, and to know the love of Christ that surpasses knowledge, that you may be filled with all the fullness of God." (Ephesians 3:14-19)

He even uses terms like "rooted" and "grounded." Paul knows that apart from Jesus, we are going to fail!

Let's look back at this lonely, disconnected scion clipping again. Is it going to make it? No, but what if it really wanted to make it, would that change anything? What if it was super nice to all the other clippings in the greenhouse? What if this clipping somehow made its way to another gardeners table once a week and sat there? Would it change the outcome? No, even though this clipping, with all it's might, wants to survive, apart from the root system, it will die. This is a reminder to us that all our good works, our mission trips, our charitable giving, and even our attendance record at our local church will not sustain us spiritually. The only way we will thrive spiritually is to be grafted into Jesus, abiding in the Holy Spirit as our nutrient source. Our family's faith won't graft us into Jesus, it must be our own personal connection. That's what abiding looks like, a healthy clipping, grafted into the Eternal Life giving root that is Jesus.

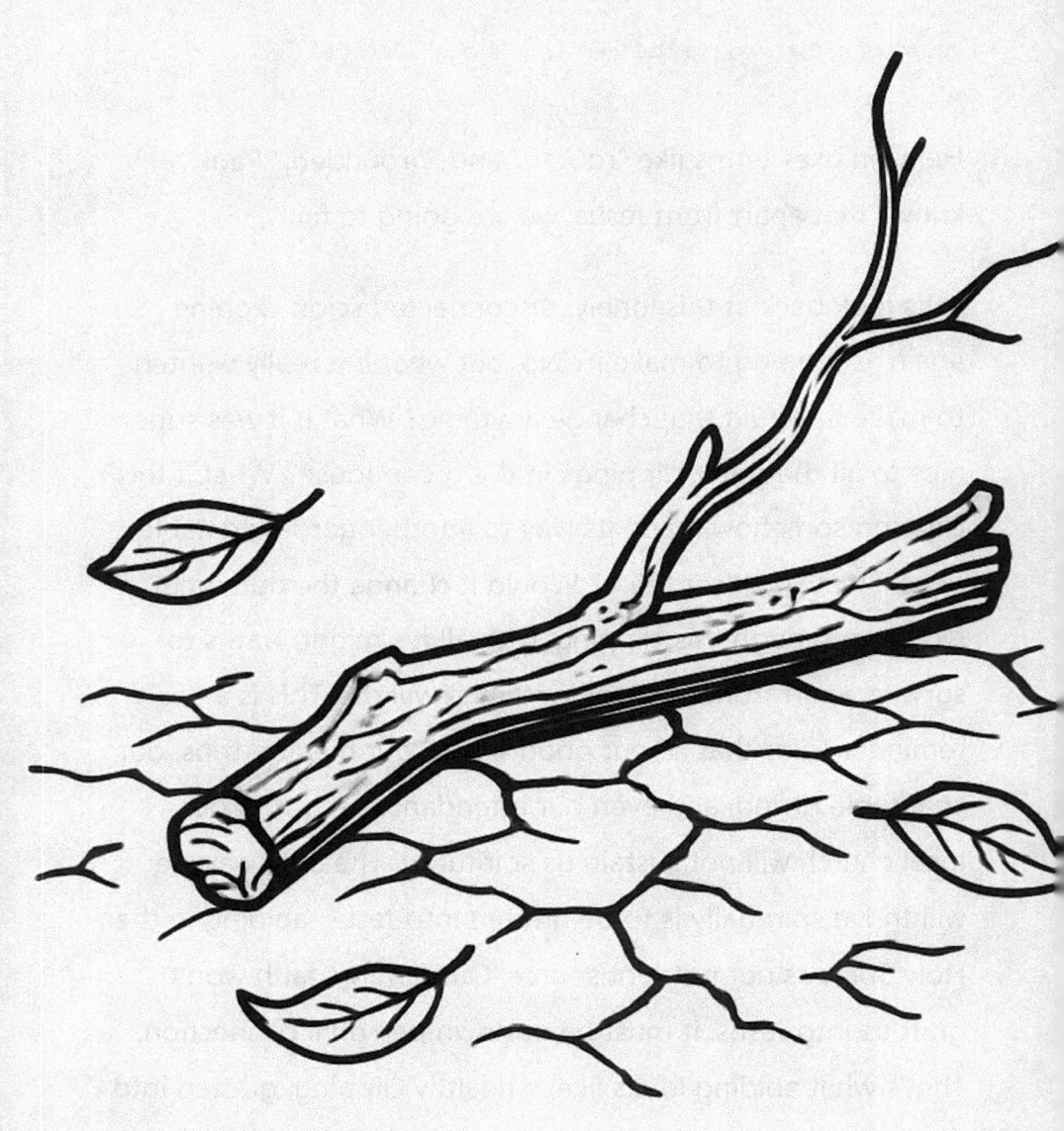

Chapter 6
Abide In His Name

One of the biggest things we must get past when sharing our faith is the fear of rejection. Jesus told us the world would reject Him, and if we are abiding in Him, then we will face the same rejection. Not because we didn't use the right words to share Jesus, but because the world is against the standard that Jesus set. If we aren't getting push back from the world, we need to ask ourselves if we are living clearly enough for Jesus. *If we don't look different than the world, what are we abiding in?*

After surrendering our lives to Jesus, our citizenship changes. We aren't part of the world anymore; we are Kingdom citizens just passing through and hopefully making the circles where God has planted us better because of our presence as we try to live out Jesus. That call is going to put a target on us. But we aren't meant to carry that target alone and deal with the attacks in our own strength. That's why Jesus sent the Holy Spirit to live in us.

Jump down to **verses 26-27**, reread these two verses.

"But when the Helper comes, whom I will send to you from the Father, the Spirit of truth, who proceeds from the Father, he will bear witness about me. And you also will bear witness, because you have been with me from the beginning. (John 15:26-27)

How does this give us confidence in the face of persecution?

In the face of persecution, there is a temptation to distance ourselves from the world. It's easier that way. We don't have the constant character attacks and disappointments, but how are we going to bear fruit in this life if we remove ourselves from it? That's where the Holy Spirit comes in. He gives us protection and, at the same time, the Holy Spirit is the source of strength. In the last series we did, GIFTED, we talked about Spiritual Gifts which are given to us by the Holy Spirit. He's not just there as a protective wall around us, He also energizes us to produce fruit that is going to last. *If we are called to bear fruit in this life, what do we have to do?* We need to first get out of the church building and into the world.

We must live to a higher standard than the world, but without coming across as judgmental. We also must lovingly speak truth into a world that not only wants to ignore the concept of truth, but they are also passionately against God. To bear fruit in this life, is not an easy task and while every generation has its challenges, your generation has unique challenges to face, but anything is possible with God.

If you noticed we jumped over a part of this passage, good for you. This middle part is difficult to understand at face value. But as good students of the Word, we are going to dig deeper. Too many people will often skip over the hard-to-understand parts of Scripture and in the process miss out on truth that is crucial to abiding in Jesus. So, let's reread **verses 22-25**. *When you read this section, what do you hear?* Try to sum up the passage in one sentence. *If Jesus had not come to earth, would mankind not be guilty of their sin?* If you only brush over this part of the passage you might make that mistake, but when we read Scripture, we must look at the fullness of the Bible and not just a single sentence or verse. *What do we know about our sin?* That everyone has sinned, Romans 3:23, that sin brings spiritual death, Romans 6:23, and that in God's mercy, He sent Jesus to pay the sin debt we owe. Jesus doesn't bring the burden of sin to an innocent people, because none of us are innocent. Instead He brings the only path to a right relationship with God the Father.

What He's saying here in John 15 is that if He had not entered our world and lived out the standard that God set before us to perfection, we might have gone on in our blind self-righteousness thinking we were doing a good job in life. The religious leaders in the New Testament struggled with this concept, they thought they were better than everyone else because of their obedience to religion. Jesus spoke to that false confidence several times.

What names did Jesus use for the religious leaders He came across? Would we have been any different if Jesus hadn't shown us our need for Him?

When Jesus entered our physical world, He brought to light just how far we fall short of the standard, not to make us feel horrible about ourselves, but to bring us to a point where we realize we aren't good enough and we need a savior. Then He went to the cross as that savior so that our sins could be forgiven.

As we wrap up this series on John 15, what does it mean to you to "abide in Jesus?"

How do you live daily in His Life, Love, and Name?

What changes can you make to bear even more fruit for the Kingdom?

What kind of pushback can you expect when you really start "abiding?"

I hope you have enjoyed this journey through John 15 as much as I did studying and preparing for it! This metaphor has been especially encouraging when facing those tough days. Knowing I'm not in this alone, that not only do I have hope, I have a helper that is walking through the valley with me! I must constantly remind myself that I'm just a branch grafted into a vine that created everything there is. I don't have to be strong enough...HE IS!

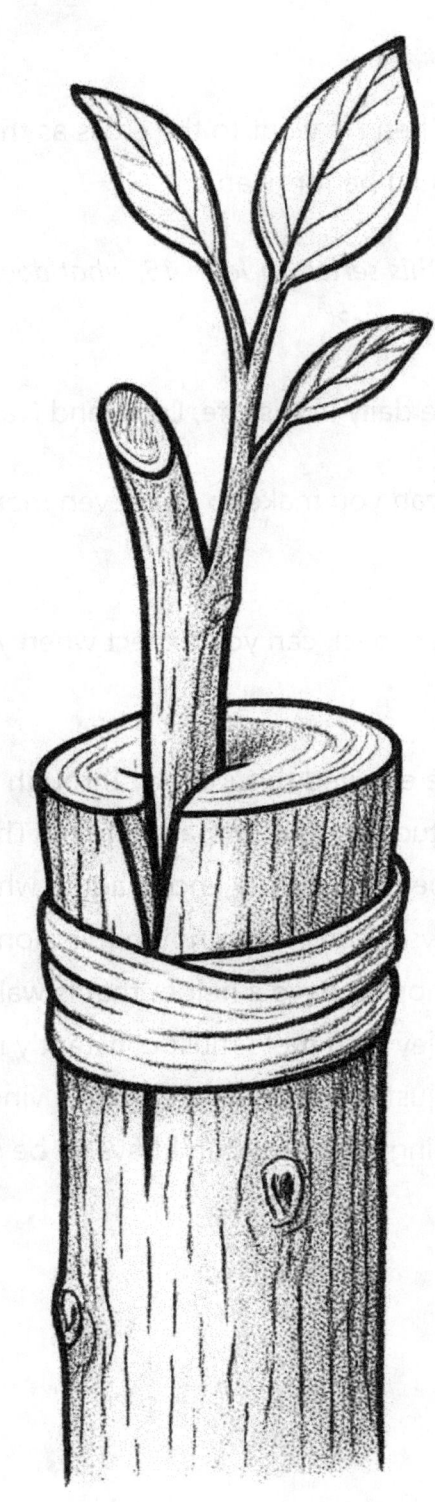

About the Author

Eric Summers has served as a dedicated student pastor for over 20 years, walking alongside young people as they navigate faith, life, and purpose. Beyond the church walls, Eric is a committed husband and the proud father of three amazing children who continually inspire and challenge him to lead by example. An avid soccer coach and lifelong athlete, he brings the same energy and discipline to the field as he does to ministry. Eric is also an active member of the F3 fitness community and a passionate rucker, always pushing himself and others to grow stronger—physically, mentally, and spiritually. Whether in the locker room, on the trail, or at the pulpit, Eric leads with heart, humility, and an unshakable belief in the power of **functional faith**.

Acknowledgments

First and foremost, I thank God for the gift of Jesus—my Savior, my strength, and the foundation of everything I am and everything I do. His grace continues to guide, sustain, and transform me daily.

To my incredible wife and our amazing children—thank you for your unwavering love, patience, and support. You are my greatest blessing and constant reminder of God's goodness. Your encouragement has been the anchor that steadies me and the fuel that keeps me moving forward.

I'm deeply grateful for the many mentors who have poured into my life over the years. Your wisdom, honesty, and willingness to challenge me have sharpened me in ways I'll never fully be able to repay. You've shaped the man, leader, and follower of Christ I am today.

To the pastors I'm honored to serve alongside—thank you for your partnership in ministry and your shared passion for reaching others with truth and love. It's a privilege to walk this calling together.

And to my F3 brothers—those I meet with in the gloom—thank you for pushing me to be better, stronger, and more faithful in every area of life. Your accountability and camaraderie are gifts I never take for granted.

Each of you has played a part in this journey, and I am thankful beyond words.

Thanks for reading! Please add a short review on Amazon and let me know what you thought! As I have been writing material for students for almost 20 years, this is just the first installment! More to come soon!